What Would YOU Do?

The Alamo

Would YOU Join the Fight?

Elaine Landau

Enslow Elementary

an imprint of

Enslow Publishers, Inc.

40 Industrial Road
Box 398
Berkeley Heights, NJ 07922
USA

http://www.enslow.com

Enslow Elementary, an imprint of Enslow Publishers, Inc.
Enslow Elementary® is a registered trademark of Enslow Publishers, Inc.

Library of Congress Cataloging-in-Publication Data

Landau, Elaine.
    The Alamo : would you join the fight? / Elaine Landau.
        pages cm. — (What would you do?)
    Includes index.
    Summary: "Explore an important event in US history. Readers decide what they would do, and then find out
        what really happened"—Provided by publisher.
    ISBN 978-0-7660-4226-1
    1. Alamo (San Antonio, Tex.)—Siege, 1836—Juvenile literature. I. Title.
    F390.L24 2014
    976.4'03—dc23
                        2013014026

Future editions:
Paperback ISBN: 978-1-4644-0395-8
EPUB ISBN: 978-1-4645-1217-9
Single-User PDF ISBN: 978-1-4646-1217-6
Multi-User PDF ISBN: 978-0-7660-5849-1

Printed in the United States of America

052014 Lake Book Manufacturing, Inc., Melrose Park, IL

10 9 8 7 6 5 4 3 2 1

To Our Readers: We have done our best to make sure all Internet Addresses in this book were active and appropriate when we went to press. However, the author and the publisher have no control over and assume no liability for the material available on those Internet sites or on other Web sites they may link to. Any comments or suggestions can be sent by e-mail to comments@enslow.com or to the address on the back cover.

♻ Enslow Publishers, Inc., is committed to printing our books on recycled paper. The paper in every book contains 10% to 30% post-consumer waste (PCW). The cover board on the outside of each book contains 100% PCW. Our goal is to do our part to help young people and the environment too!

Every effort has been made to locate all copyright holders of material used in this book. If any errors or omissions have occurred, corrections will be made in future editions of this book.

Illustration Credits: ©Clipart.com, pp. 27, 33, 37(right); Contributor Larry D. Moore/Wikipedia.com, p. 17; ©Corel Corporation, p. 44; *The Dictionary of American Portraits*, published by Dover Publications, Inc., in 1967, pp. 11(both) ©Enslow Publishers, Inc., pp. 8, 27, 34, 43; Library of Congress, pp. 1, 15, 18, 19, 20, 29, 30, 41, 42; ©1990 PhotoDisc, Inc., p. 23; Shutterstock.com, (©Dallas Events Inc, p. 6, ©Stocksnapper, p. 7); Texas Department of Transportation, p. 38; ©Thinkstock: Rob Shone, p. 12; University of Texas Libraries, p. 4; Wikipedia.com Public Domain image, pp. 16, 37(left)

Cover Illustration: Library of Congress

Contents

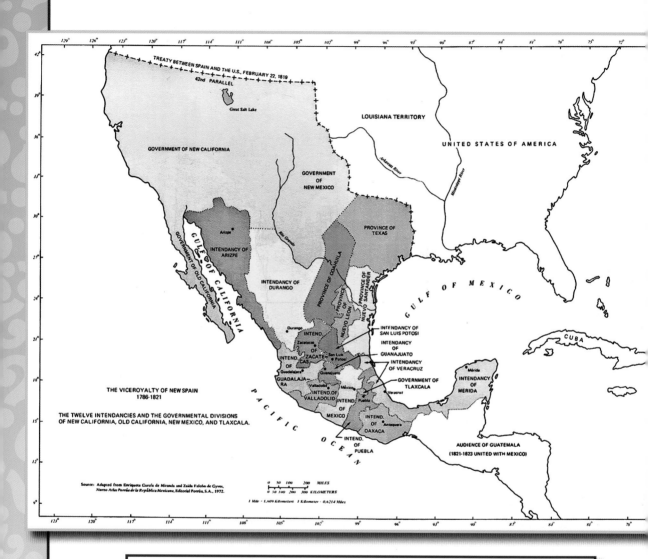

This is a map of New Spain showing the borders from 1786–1821. Most of New Spain eventually became Mexico.

A Chance for Change

The early 1800s was an exciting time. The United States was still a very new country. There were large areas of unsettled land to the west. Some Americans longed to claim and tame those areas.

The land we know today as Texas was fertile, large, and open. Yet back then it didn't belong to the United States. It belonged to Spain. Texas and the area we know today as Mexico were part of a Spanish settlement called New Spain. Most of the Spanish settlers made their home in Mexico. Only a small number of them lived to the north in Texas.

There weren't just Spanish settlers living in what would later be Texas. There were also some American Indian tribes. Among these were the Comanche and

Although seemingly empty to the first white settlers, Texas was home to American Indian tribes and plenty of wildlife. The vast land held many dangers for the settlers.

the Apache. These Indians did not stay in one place for long. They roamed the land following the buffalo.

Spain also allowed some Americans into New Spain. Those who came had to obey the colony's laws. As there were few settlers, there were also few roads or stores. A doctor or dentist might be hundreds of miles or more away.

Yet some Americans still wanted to be there. They wanted to build homes, plant crops, and raise cattle. There was plenty of timber and grazing land too. The Americans felt that anything might be possible there.

The Comanche were wanderers who lived off the land. Warriors on horseback hunted the plentiful game using bow and arrow skillfully.

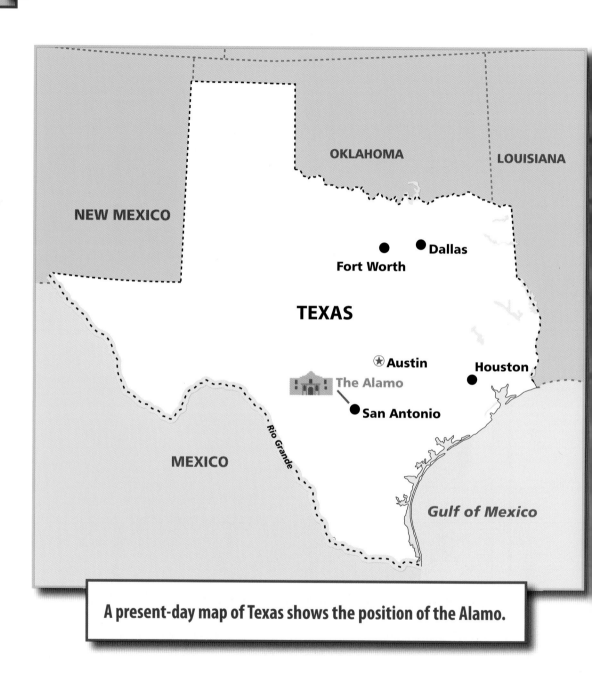

A present-day map of Texas shows the position of the Alamo.

What Would YOU Do?

❀ Would you move to New Spain to become a new land owner? *OR* . . .

❀ Would you stay in the United States and live in a more settled place? Keep in mind that you could stay in the United States and become a new land owner without remaining in a settled place. There was plenty of wilderness in what then was the United States—the entire Louisiana Territory, or even the Old Northwest Territory east of the Mississippi.

Off to New Spain

Some people from the United States settled in New Spain. They might have been an especially adventurous bunch. Others chose not to go.

Most of the Spanish settlers in New Spain lived south of where the Americans settled. As of 1810, the Spanish settlers went to war against Spain. The colony of New Spain wanted its independence. It was a long and bloody struggle. New Spain did not win until 1821. Then the entire area was known as Mexico.

For years, Mexico was in an uproar due to the war. The new government had paid little attention to the few American settlers in Texas or the northern part of New Spain. Yet a Missouri banker named Moses Austin and his son Stephen changed things. They did a lot to bring more people from the United States there. They felt that developing the area would benefit everyone. From 1821 on, Stephen Austin brought over 1,500 Americans into New Spain.

Yet going to Texas wasn't easy. The American settlers had to follow strict rules. They had to become

Moses Austin, a Missouri banker, asked the Spanish government in San Antonio to allow him to bring Americans to settle there.

Stephen Austin followed through on his father's dream of leading Americans to colonize Texas.

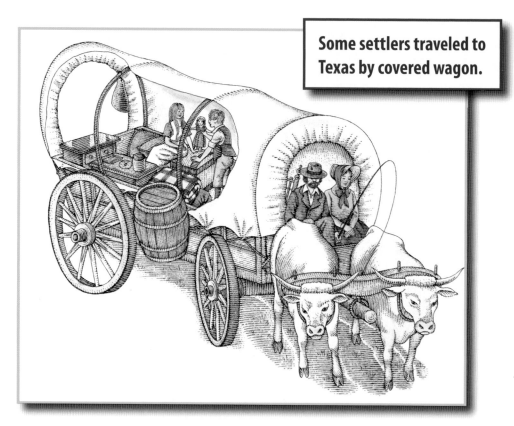

Some settlers traveled to Texas by covered wagon.

Catholics. They also had to give up being American citizens. They could not bring slaves. New settlers had to become Spanish citizens before the Mexicans won the war for independence. After the war, they had to become Mexican citizens. There were also rules for proper behavior. Heavy drinking, swearing, and gambling were not permitted. Yet most of the settlers were hearty pioneers who did not mind the rules. They were glad they came.

What Would YOU Do?

✿ Would you give up being an American citizen for a good piece of land? *OR* . . .

✿ Would you turn your back on the lure of free land? Would being an American mean too much to you to give up?

Life Down Mexico Way

Some Americans became Mexican citizens to get prime land. They hoped to do well and were just there for profit. For a while, this was fine.

By 1835, things changed. A brutal man named General Antonio López de Santa Anna had become Mexico's president in 1833. Santa Anna cared little about the freedoms the American settlers had enjoyed in the United States. Under Santa Anna, the settlers didn't have the right to elect their own officials. They also weren't promised fair and open jury trials.

Santa Anna did not want streams of Americans coming to Texas. He was afraid they might become too powerful. Many American settlers had already begun to think that Texas should be free of Mexico. They spoke about rebelling. If they won the rebellion, Texas would not be part of Mexico any longer. It would not be part of the United States either. It would be a separate nation.

General Antonio López de Santa Anna was president of Mexico eleven times. He led the Mexican Army in its attack of the Alamo.

The first armed conflict between the rebels and the Mexicans broke out in 1835. The town of Gonzales in Texas had a small cannon. Sometimes the settlers used it to scare off American Indians.

The Mexicans wanted to take the canon. So a band of Mexican soldiers was sent to Gonzales to get it. This made the American settlers in the town really angry. Two women were ready to do their part to save the cannon. They wrote the words COME AND TAKE IT in bold letters on one of their wedding gowns. Then they hung the dress on the canon.

The men fired the cannon at the Mexican soldiers when they arrived. That sent them back home without the canon. The shot became known as "The First Shot of the Texas Revolution."

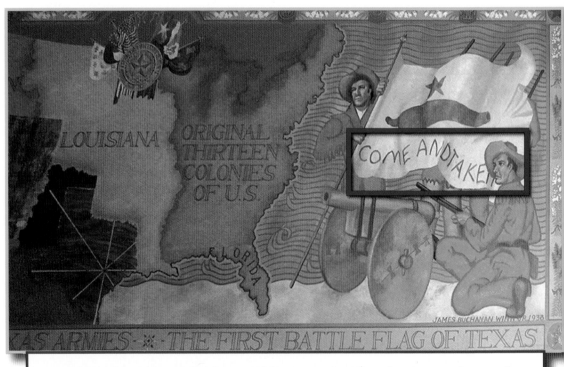

A mural at the Gonzales Memorial Museum in Gonzales, Texas shows the American settlers with the COME AND TAKE IT flag draped over a cannon.

This cannon, displayed at the Gonzales Memorial Museum in Gonzales, Texas, may have started the battle.

What Would YOU Do?

❀ Would you join the rebels in Gonzales? *OR* . . .

❀ Would you let the Mexicans have the cannon? You are making a good living where you are. Are you really ready to go to war?

Troubling Times

By now, few American settlers were against going to war. Most wanted independence. In November 1835, many of them gathered at the town of San Felipe. They came to plan the fight ahead. At that meeting an outstanding leader arose. His name was Sam Houston. He would help the settlers try to win their freedom.

In the fight for Texan independence, Sam Houston played a leading role. He was president of the Republic of Texas for two terms. He also served as governor and senator of the state.

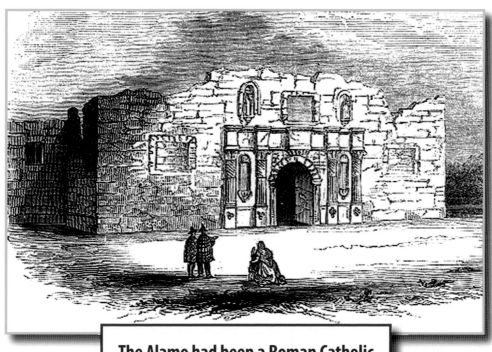

The Alamo had been a Roman Catholic mission before it was used as a fort.

Meanwhile Mexico's president, Santa Anna, found out about the settlers' rebellion. He was furious. He wanted to put the settlers in their place. Santa Anna sent his brother-in-law, General Martin Perfecto de Cos, north to Texas to do so.

In December 1835, General Cos arrived in San Antonio and occupied the Alamo. The Alamo was first built as a mission. Later, it was used as a fort.

Martin Perfecto de Cos commanded Mexican troops in Texas.

Cos talked tough but was not a good general. He came with a force of 1,500 well trained Mexican soldiers. But they were soon defeated by just about 300 Texas rebels. Now the rebels took over the Alamo. Yet they felt there would be more trouble.

They were right. Santa Anna put together a Mexican army of thousands of soldiers and headed north with them. Santa Anna thought of the rebel soldiers as traitors. One thing was certain. Blood would be shed. No one would ever forget this fight.

What Would YOU Do?

What if you were Mexican President Santa Anna?

❀ Would you deal harshly with the rebels? *OR* . . .

❀ Would you try to work out things with the rebels? That way, lives on both sides would be saved.

To Fight or Flee

Santa Anna did not want peace. He wanted the rebels punished. He hoped to make an example of them.

The rebel troops badly needed training. Most of these men had never served in a formal army. They'd only fought off some American Indian raids.

The rebel soldiers also didn't have many supplies. They brought blankets, bullets, and some food from home. Some of the men rounded up about thirty head of cattle. They herded them into the Alamo. This would supply them with beef for a while. They also took bushels of corn to the fort.

This is how the Alamo looks today.

But while some settlers stayed to defend the Alamo, others did not want to. Some of these people were farmers, ranchers, and merchants. They felt that the battle for the Alamo could not be won. The odds against the rebels were just too great. Santa Anna had far more soldiers and weapons.

Those who considered leaving were not proud of the idea of going. They knew they were badly needed. Yet they were not ready to die for what they believed was a hopeless cause.

What Would YOU Do?

✿ **Would you stay and defend the Alamo? You would be taking an important stand. *OR* . . .**

✿ **Would you quickly leave the area? You can't help Texas become independent if you die.**

On the Other Side

Many able-bodied men left the area. They felt the Alamo could not be saved. Only about 150 settlers stayed to defend it.

On the other side, Santa Anna's men were not in the best place either. Many of these soldiers had been forced into service. The Mexican army also had too many officers and not enough fighters. There were more men who wanted to give orders than do battle.

The trip north to the Alamo was difficult. General Santa Anna was in a great hurry to get there. He did not take the time to supply his men with enough food, warm clothing, medical supplies or weapons.

Mexican troops prepare to attack the Alamo.

He didn't even bring a doctor along. There was no help for the men who became sick or hurt.

The winter was unusually cold that year. Freezing winds made the men shiver as they marched. Many died during the trip to the Alamo. Some thought they might be better off deserting than fighting.

What Would YOU Do?

If you were a Mexican soldier:

❀ **Would you march on to the Alamo?** *OR ...*

❀ **Would you try to sneak off without being seen?**

Who Will Lead the Rebel Soldiers?

While some Mexican soldiers deserted, most did not. Yet different groups of soldiers arrived at the Alamo at different times. So Santa Anna waited before launching a full attack.

He used this time to stage the siege of the Alamo. First, he surrounded the fort. Next, he had a number of trenches dug. These would be used to move men and weapons closer to the fort. He also fired cannons at all hours. This helped disturb the rebels' sleep.

Santa Anna had no idea that there were so few rebel soldiers within the Alamo.

He also didn't know that his enemy faced leadership problems as well. There were three outstanding leaders inside the Alamo. They had different fighting styles. At first no one was quite sure who'd take the lead.

One of the men was Jim Bowie. Bowie was skilled with a gun and a knife. Bowie also had personal appeal. Men would follow him in a fight.

Another possible leader was William Barret Travis. Travis was a formally trained soldier who could lead an army. He wanted to direct the fight at the Alamo.

Jim Bowie was a colorful frontiersman who became a legendary hero of the Texas Revolution.

William Barret Travis was one hero of the battle of the Alamo. He was a courageous and devoted leader.

Davy Crockett boosted the morale of the men at the Alamo when he volunteered to fight alongside them against Santa Anna's army. Crockett is shown in a cloth hunting outfit and a board-brimmed hat, not the legendary buckskins and coonskin cap.

The famous frontiersman Davy Crockett also came to the Alamo. There were all sorts of legends about Crockett. He was known to be brave. He wore a coonskin cap and had a rifle he named Old Betsy.

Of the three, Bowie and Travis were the ones most interested in being in charge. They argued quite a bit over this.

What Would YOU Do?

If you had to choose a leader for the Alamo battle:

✺ **Would you pick Jim Bowie? He was a colorful character known for his bravery. *OR . . .***

✺ **Would you pick William Barret Travis—a well trained soldier who knew how to lead an army?**

Before the Attack

Travis and Bowie worked things out between them. Because of his military background, Travis would command the experienced soldiers. Bowie would be in charge of the volunteers. Yet in the months before 1836, Bowie became very ill. So Travis was largely in charge of defending the Alamo.

There was lots to do before Santa Anna's full-scale attack. The men made large holes in the inside walls of the Alamo's various buildings. This would let the men quickly move about if the enemy got over the wall. The men also broke up old horseshoes, chains, and other metal objects. They would use this as ammunition for their cannon.

This antique cannon is on display at the Alamo. Cannons played a big part in each battle of the conflict between the Texans and the Mexican Army.

There was more to be done as well. But Travis felt that nothing really mattered if more troops didn't come soon. Every night Travis secretly sent out messengers on horseback. The message they carried was brief but vital. Travis argued that more men had to come right away. Without more troops, the battle for the Alamo was doomed.

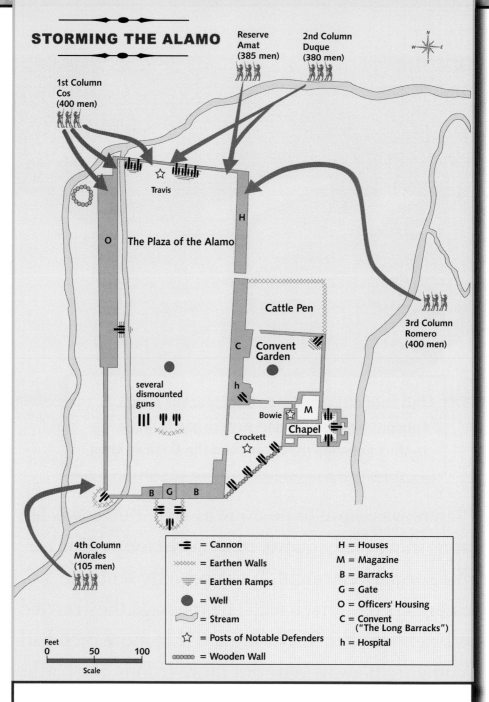

STORMING THE ALAMO

Reserve Amat (385 men)

2nd Column Duque (380 men)

1st Column Cos (400 men)

Travis

H

O   The Plaza of the Alamo

Cattle Pen

3rd Column Romero (400 men)

C   Convent Garden

h

several dismounted guns

Bowie   M

Crockett   Chapel

B G B

4th Column Morales (105 men)

= Cannon
= Earthen Walls
= Earthen Ramps
= Well
= Stream
= Posts of Notable Defenders
= Wooden Wall

H = Houses
M = Magazine
B = Barracks
G = Gate
O = Officers' Housing
C = Convent ("The Long Barracks")
h = Hospital

Feet
0   50   100
Scale

Since it was originally a mission, the Alamo was not intended to be used as a fort. The men inside the Alamo hastily prepared for its defense by placing cannons in strategic positions.

Months before, Sam Houston had sent Jim Bowie to blow up the Alamo. Santa Anna could not capture what wasn't there. Bowie decided to defend the fort instead. Yet would Travis be wise to blow it up now and make Santa Anna look foolish?

What Would YOU Do?

❀ If you were Travis, would you blow up the Alamo now? *OR . . .*

❀ Would you wait for more soldiers to arrive and hope for the best?

Attack!

Like Jim Bowie, Travis did not blow up the Alamo. The fort had become an important symbol of Texan independence. Travis kept sending out pleas for help. But only a small number of men answered his call. There were fewer than two hundred men ready to defend the Alamo.

A huge number of Mexican soldiers, probably between 2,000 and 4,000, were under Santa Anna's command. These soldiers were ready to attack the fort on March 5, 1836.

Santa Anna did not have to cause a blood bath. There was another choice. The rebels did not have very much food. The Mexican troops could remain camped outside the Alamo. After a few weeks or less, the rebels would be starving. They would have to give up.

Many of the volunteers dressed in buckskins and armed themselves with muskets or Kentucky long rifles.

This is what a Mexican soldier would have looked like at the time of the battle of the Alamo. All infantrymen wore a black shako—the stiff, cylindrical hat popular at the time—with a brass plate and small red plume.

This diorama re-creates the scene at the Alamo as Mexican soldiers stand ready to attack. The diorama was created from studies done by historians and accounts of survivors.

What Would YOU Do?

❀ **Would you attack the Alamo with brutal force?** *OR* . . .

❀ **Would you wait until the rebels' food ran out?**

Their Dream Came True

Santa Anna attacked with all his might. He showed the rebels no mercy. The Mexicans used cannon fire and muskets to bring down the rebels. At times, the soldiers fought face to face on the ground with bayonets—large knives that fit onto the ends of rifles.

The rebels fought bravely. Even though they were losing the battle, they did not desert their posts. They tried to win but died doing it. Travis was one of the first to be killed. Jim Bowie had been too ill to leave his bed that day. So the Mexicans killed him where he was. At the end of the battle, all of the rebels were dead. When he left there was blood everywhere. Even those who tried to surrender were killed.

This painting, called *The Battle of the Alamo*, shows Mexican soldiers closing in on a small band of Alamo defenders.

Santa Anna won the battle. Yet the fight for Texas independence was hardly over. The rebels would not give up. They now had a stirring new battle cry—it was: Remember the Alamo!

The next month Texas won its independence from Mexico. Then in July 1836, Sam Houston was elected president of the Republic of Texas. But now this new nation longed for something else. The Texans wanted

In this political cartoon, Mexican Generals Santa Anna and Cos offer their swords to Texan General Sam Houston while denying responsibility for the massacre at the Alamo. Houston's American Indian clothing may be a reference to the years he spent living with the Cherokee as a young man.

to join the United States. They were ready to be part of a large, strong, and proud nation. That dream came true for them on December 29, 1845. The stand the rebels took at the Alamo helped make this possible. The courage of those brave men and women will never be forgotten.

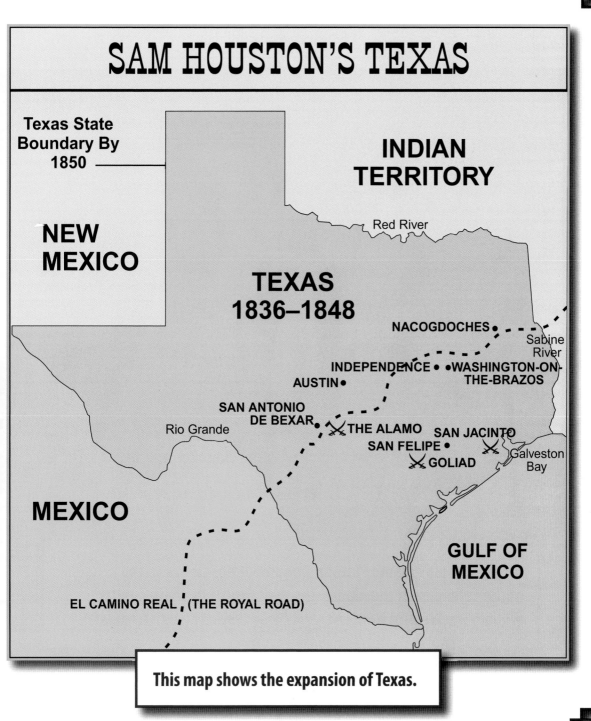

SAM HOUSTON'S TEXAS

Texas State Boundary By 1850

INDIAN TERRITORY

NEW MEXICO

Red River

TEXAS 1836–1848

NACOGDOCHES

Sabine River

INDEPENDENCE • WASHINGTON-ON-THE-BRAZOS

AUSTIN •

SAN ANTONIO DE BEXAR •

Rio Grande

THE ALAMO

SAN JACINTO

SAN FELIPE •

Galveston Bay

GOLIAD

MEXICO

GULF OF MEXICO

EL CAMINO REAL (THE ROYAL ROAD)

This map shows the expansion of Texas.

In San Antonio's Alamo Plaza, a monument has been erected in honor of the defenders of the Alamo. The west face of the base depicts William Travis (third from left) and David Crockett (sixth from left).

Timeline

1810—Spanish settlers in New Spain go to war with Spain for their independence.

1821—New Spain wins its independence from Spain.

1833—General Santa Anna becomes Mexico's president.

1835 *(October)*—The first armed conflict between Mexico and the American rebels breaks out at the town of Gonzales.

1835 *(November)*—American rebels meet at the town of San Felipe to plan their fight against Mexico for independence.

1835 *(December)*—Texans attack the Mexican Army led by General Cos. The Mexicans surrender.

1836 *(February)*—Mexican Army arrives at San Antonio and occupies the town. The siege of the Alamo begins.

1836 *(March)*—General Santa Anna attacks the Alamo and defeats the rebel forces.

1836 *(April)*—Houston's army defeats Santa Anna's forces at the Battle of San Jancinto.

1836 *(July)*—Sam Houston is elected president of the Republic of Texas.

1845 *(December)*—Texas becomes part of the United States.

Words to Know

ammunition—Things that can be fired from a weapon, such as bullets or arrows.

bayonet—A long knife that can fit on the end of a rifle.

fort—A strongly built building that can survive attacks.

mission—A church or other place where a religious order lives.

musket—A gun with a long barrel that was used before rifles were invented.

post—A place where someone on military duty remains.

rebels—People who fight against those in charge.

siege—A military move in which an enemy surrounds a fort or castle cutting off supplies to the people inside.

surrender—To give up.

timber—Cut wood used for building.

traitor—A person who is disloyal.

troops—Soldiers.

Learn More

Books

Burgan, Michael. *The Alamo.* New York: Chelsea House Publications, 2009.

Downey, Tika. *Texas: the Lone Star State.* New York: Powerkids Press, 2010.

Levy, Janey. *The Battle of the Alamo.* New York: Powerhouse Press, 2009.

Murphy, Jim. *Inside the Alamo.* New York: Delacorte Press, 2003.

Nelson, Kristin L. *The Alamo.* Minneapolis, Minn.: Lerner, 2011.

Turner, Carolyn. *Sam Houston.* New York: Weigl Publishers, 2011.

Walker, Paul Robert. *Remember the Alamo: Texians, Tejanos, and Mexicans Tell Their Stories.* Washington, D.C.: National Geographic Children's Books, 2007.

Web Sites

The Alamo
<http://www.thealamo.org>

Lone Star Junction: Davy Crockett
<http://www.lsjunction.com/people/crockett.htm>

Index